How to Outsource

Steve Coast

Contents

1 Introduction

The idea of outsourcing is very easy – find people to do work for us because we can't do it or we don't have the time. The reality is *much* more complicated…

Are you scared or intimidated of outsourcing your work? You should be. It's easy to waste time, money and valuable resources when you go about it the wrong way. With some help, you can avoid the common mistakes and get going much more quickly.

First, you should know *what to outsource*. At first glance this sounds easy but really, you need to know what you're good at (and not so good at) so you know what others can do better, faster or cheaper than you can. Most of us think we're good at everything, or we'd like to think so. We need to be honest and realize we aren't good at all things all the time. Your first step is to recognize this is a great thing, and make your life better by letting go of and outsourcing the other things.

Second, you need to figure out *who to outsource to*. What type of person can help with your project? What skills do they need? When does it need to be done? This isn't always easy to answer. Think about it, if we aren't good at something then how do we judge if someone else is going to help?

Third, *how and where do you find them?* There are a variety of ways to find people for different tasks. They can be geographically near or far, work on your project goal or some tiny piece of it. They can work exclusively for you or part-time, amongst many other options.

This little book is about how to answer these questions and get you on your way!

Just so we're all clear, this isn't a technical book. If you need technical help get in touch or find someone near you (or outsource them!)

Who am I?

I'm Steve Coast and I founded and built much of the OpenStreetMap project, a kind of Wikipedia of maps. Over time I've spent hundreds of thousands of dollars outsourcing work. I work as a coach and advisor to many others who outsource millions of dollars more.

Let me know what you think of the book, my email is steve@stevecoast.com.

2 What to Outsource

If you already have a simple, well-defined problem or project to outsource you can of course skip this section. If you don't, read on…

What are you good at?

The most wonderful job is;

a) Something you're good at,
b) you enjoy and
c) pays well.

It's easier to have two or one out of the three. If you know what you're good at, then it becomes much easier to figure out what you're *not* good at.

Grab a piece of paper and write down what you think you're good at. Most of us have never done this, it's worth the time.

As humans, we're full of blind spots and we don't always know ourselves as well as we think we do. Because of this, it can be easier to ask other people what we're good at. Ask five people what they think you're good at and write it down.

Try to ask them in a way that doesn't bias the answer. If you ask people "what do you think I'm good at?" They'll try to tell you what you want to hear. They'll ask you what you mean, or what area you're interested in. Because of this, first frame the question.

Ask them to assume there is no right or wrong answer, and you're trying to understand your strengths to figure out what to work on. Make sure to ask many different people, and try to talk to people that aren't biased, like your immediate family. People that know you well, like long-time coworkers are a great example of someone to ask.

The answers you hear may surprise you, and may be outside of what you're thinking.

For example, you might be told that you're a good listener, but your job is in robotics. Don't argue with the list. Look for the things on the list that you hear multiple times from different people.

Great – got a list of strengths and things you're good at?

The list you're building is important, don't skip it! This is one of those things where you should really do the work: This doesn't work well as a theoretical exercise.

What do you enjoy?

Take the list you've made, and look at all the thing's you're good at. Whether you agree or disagree with them, circle the ones that you enjoy.

What makes money?

Take the same list, and highlight the ones that also can make money. If you don't have a highlighter, then underline or something else to mark the items.

Analyzing the results

Look at the final list of *strengths*: items that meet both requirements of enjoyment and making money. If you have a few things that you're good at, you enjoy and make money that's wonderful!

To think about some items with one or two out of three, here are some examples to help you:

Strengths	Good At	Thinking	Suggestion
Good at it	Listening	Is there a way you can enjoy it and make money?	Become a therapist
Enjoy it	Mountain Biking	Can you get good at it and make money?	Work at a bike shop
Good at it **and** enjoy it	Horse Riding	How can you make money?	Write a blog about topics you come across, advertise on it and find clients using it
Good at it **and** make money doing it	Knitting Sweaters (for many people if they're paid and good at it but don't enjoy it, it's their day job)	How can you enjoy it?	Hire other people to knit the sweaters so you can focus on the parts you enjoy. In other

			words – outsource this.
Enjoy it **and** make money doing it (but not good at it)	*This category usually doesn't exist since if people are paying you, then you're good at it.*	How can you get good at it?	Do you have imposter syndrome?
Make money doing it	Your 'day job'	How can you enjoy it and be good at it?	Since you know how to do it, hiring people to do this is usually easy

Notice you usually have a choice for each item. You can either change yourself (find a way to enjoy it, for example) or find someone else to do it, or you can do both.

For all the things not on the list, find someone else to do it. If cleaning toilets isn't on your list, find someone else to do it.

For the things you enjoy, are good at and make money, do lots of this! This is the trifecta, spend your time doing these things.

For everything else, find someone else to do it.

The flip side

If you enjoy doing something, potentially you can ruin the fun by turning it in to work. Figure skating on the weekend is unlikely to get more enjoyable, if you start selling skates all day.

In the same way, not caring about what you work on can be very useful. Bank loan officers are looking for people who want to make money as their first consideration, not people pursuing a project for fun or because it's a passion.

Not caring about running car washes or running a painting company is different from not caring about the quality of the work. To make money, it should be the best car wash or paint shop in town.

What are you spending your time on?

You can easily be spending your time on the wrong things.

The classic example is bookkeeping and accounts. You're great at selling snowboards, but spend a day each month bookkeeping. That day is better spent selling snowboards, or going to a sales training event to get better, or practically doing anything other than bookkeeping.

Write down how you think you spent your time last week. Now this week, track it. Use a pen and paper if you must. Usually, how you think you spent your time and how you actually spent it are different.

When you look at all the ways you spent your time, how many of these correlate to your original list of things you enjoy, are good at or make money?

Circle all the things you don't enjoy, don't make money on, or aren't good at that you did last week. *These are things to outsource.*

The Secret
People enjoy doing the things you don't enjoy.

Accounting may be incredibly boring to you – all those numbers! But there are people who love it. We often assume that if we don't enjoy doing something, then everyone else must loathe doing it as well. We enjoy and surround ourselves with people like ourselves, we don't often meet those other people who enjoy doing what we don't enjoy.

But there is proof. Just go look on the internet. There are people who love almost anything you can imagine, including cleaning sewers. Or kite surfing. Or colonoscopies. Or making their own toasters.

Here's the double secret: *Because they love it (doing what you don't like) they will do it better, cheaper, and quicker than you can.*

It's incredible, but true. You should try to focus on what you make money at, which is usually what you're good at. For everything else, it's better, cheaper and quicker to hire someone else.

This is where prosperity comes from. In economics, we call this *specialization of labor*. You do what you're good at, and hire other people to do what they're good at.

There are two other big reasons you want to hire someone.

First, they know things you don't know. Here's an example: It's very common for engineers to think of a legal document as instructions, a recipe, or software. The reason you pay a lawyer is that it's the opposite in reality, and a lawyer knows this. Sales people know how to sell, lawyers know the law, and so on.

Second, they know people you don't know. You hire PR people because they have a network of journalists and editors they know, not because they're good at PR (though that's great too).

While you can learn what you don't know, and you can meet people you don't know, it will take you a long time, cost you money and you might not enjoy it. It's better, cheaper and quicker to find someone else who already has the knowledge or the network of people to get something done.

Open thinking about people with other skills

When you think about people with other skillsets, understand they probably think differently about things. They will likely have a different thought process and approach.

I've seen it many times at software companies. The engineers think the sales people are somewhere between pointless and useless. The sales people think the engineers should be outsourced to Timbuktu.

This is because their skillsets are almost mutually exclusive. Engineers deal in logic all day long. Sales people deal in emotions all day long. So, they don't have a great understanding of each other's job. We don't want to fix that here.

What we *do* want, is for you to understand both sides.

The key is to understand that different people think differently. Let the engineers be trapped in engineering, they enjoy it. Let the sales people be trapped in sales, they enjoy that. Our job is to step up a level, because if we don't, we will try to hire sales people in to engineering and engineers in to sales.

Both engineering and sales are fun, fine vocations. There's nothing negative about either. But for you to hire people you should understand that different roles require different thinking and have different cultures. That doesn't make one better than the other.

Try to understand the role you're hiring for. What makes them tick? What conferences do they go to? Can you put yourself in their shoes?

The Problems

Here's what you're going to say:

- I don't have the **money** to hire someone
- I don't have the **time** to hire someone
- I don't know **how** to hire someone

These are reasonable and good concerns.

If you're literally bootstrapping with $0 then this is literally true. The advantage for you with $0 is you have nothing to lose. You also have everything to gain. By learning how to do things yourself with $0, you get an education no university can give you. For everyone else, read on:

I don't have the money
Yes, you do!

The key is to change how you think about money. Most of us think we're saving money by doing our own bookkeeping. We think about it in terms of plain cash – do we have the money or does someone else?

We need to change this black & white idea by remembering the other two things from our list earlier. Do we enjoy it the task, and are we good at it? For most people, the answer is no and no.

This is one of those things where the primary effect is easy to see – we save money by doing our own accounting! Yay!

What we don't see is the money we would make doing something else. We could pay a bookkeeper $50/hour to do our bookkeeping, and *at the same time* be earning $100/hour selling snowboards.

Even if we earn the same or less per-hour than our bookkeeper, it's usually better to pay them to do it. Why? Because we're not usually good at it and we don't enjoy it.

If we're not good at it, we will make mistakes. If you make a mistake in bookkeeping it will cost you real money, it's just a matter of time.

If we do not enjoy it, we are paying everywhere else in life. We're less happy, we have less energy and so on. You need happiness and energy much more than the $50, believe me. It's very draining to work on the things we don't enjoy, and the costs are hidden all over the place.

Here's the other thing: Hiring can be way, way cheaper than you expect. You may pay $50/hour to accountants where you live, but your accountant doesn't have to be where you live. They can be a lot cheaper in other towns or countries, and thanks to the internet you can hire them there instead.

I don't have the time

Not having time is one of the best reasons to hire someone: By hiring them, you get more time!

Not having time is a wonderful place to be in. Most people don't have money. If you need to have a problem, not having time is the best one to have.

We need to think about margins.

Imagine a designer who's paid $1000 to do a project and it will take 9 hours to complete it, plus one hour for a client phone call. This designer is very busy and has no time. They're paid $100/hour ($1,000 divided by 10 hours of work total).

Imagine *another* designer who's also paid $1000 for a project, but instead pays $500 to someone else to do the work for them. Now they only work one hour with the client on the phone call. They're paid $500 for that one hour. So, they're paid $500/hour and 'gain' 9 free hours. Yes, they're paid 50% less. But they did it for *90% less time!*

They could do two projects like this and spend 2 hours, still make $1000, and have 8 hours free to work or play.

Which would you pick? 10 hours for $1,000 or 2 hours for $1,000?

You may quibble that they need to spend some time with their outsourced designer, and that's fair, but it doesn't negate the point.

You may also think you don't want to outsource what you do. But consider this – if you do something well, you're going to be great at hiring for it. If you're a designer, you know what great design looks like. You'll be good at hiring designers. If you're trying to hire a nuclear physicist it could be a lot more difficult for you to make sure you're getting the best cost/quality you're looking for.

Which brings us neatly to the last objection:

I don't know how to hire

Luckily, you're reading this book! Let's continue...

3 Who To Outsource To

Now we know *what* we want outsourced, we should figure out *who* can do that work.

We can:

- Hire **nobody** at all
- Find **someone else** already employed with us
- Try to **hire a computer** for the job
- Actually, really **hire someone**

Nobody

The absolute best person to outsource work to is nobody at all.

If you look at the job or task you want to outsource, can it be avoided entirely? Here's an example: You run a restaurant and you need someone to clean the tablecloths. Can you get away with no tablecloths at all?

How about paper disposable tablecloths?

Many tasks are like this. Let's say you're doing a lot of online marketing. Are you getting any customers online or are they all walking in the door? The solution may be to just stop online marketing rather than hiring someone to do it.

The absolute classic friction point to remove is middle men. Here's an example: You're the point of contact for a company with a supplier and everyone at the company goes through you. Do they *really* need to go through you? Could people get quicker answers talking to them directly and cc you? This can open more time for you to do other work.

Have a real, deep, think about the work. Can you just avoid it in the first place?

Someone Else

The second-best person to outsource work to is someone who's already employed with you or your company.

Do you have a co-worker or friend who can do it? You may be surprised at what people enjoy doing. Maybe you have an employee who enjoys bookkeeping and has some spare time to help you. You can reallocate their energies this way to help you. Never force people in to things like this; you'll get much more out of them if they sincerely want to do it.

On a related note, volunteers can be wonderful. There are all kinds of people who enjoy volunteering to help. Maybe someone is passionate about what you're doing and would love to help you out for free. Try giving someone like that more work. The worst that can happen is they say no.

Hire a Computer

A very close third 'person' you want to hire is a computer. If you can replace some work with an automated process, you can save a lot of time and money.

Can you automate it? There are two main classes of things you can automate.

First, tasks you can automate yourself. Sending your customers reminder emails is the kind of thing that you can do *manually* every Monday for example. But, there are many tools out there to do this *automatically* for you (try MailChimp at mailchimp.com).

Maybe you have a little experience with spreadsheets, or sales tools. With a little work, you can typically automate a lot of things.

What if you personally can't or don't want to automate it? Hire someone to automate it. This requires a larger outline.

Here's the tricky thing – you don't know what you can and can't automate. *Because if you did know, then you'd already automate it or would be doing so.*

When you look at the work you have in front of you, you may think it isn't automatable. But someone in software may think it's easy to automate and *you don't know that*.

Here's an example. You often take contracts to be checked by a lawyer, but it turns out that in 80% of the cases, no changes need to be made. In many cases there are simple automated checking systems which could find the 20% that do need work, rather than paying a lawyer every time.

How many times have people told you that they couldn't do what you do? Most of us think this way about our jobs; "oh, it's easy! I just read these books and practice". The key here, is that most other people in the world feel the same way about their jobs, too. Everyone from accountants to zoologists pretty much just read books (whether in or out of school) and practiced.

So, we don't directly know what we could automate in our work. We are left unsure if we can or cannot automate it.

Therefore, we may need to ask an intermediary. Either hire someone to check if we can automate something, or show a more knowledgeable person who knows software, all the things we're doing and see if a computer can do it automatically. It may be surprising what a computer can do, in this new era of machine learning.

Yes, this will cost money up front. But the advantage is (once it is automated) it will be much cheaper to do from then onward. Both with your time and your money.

It took a lot of time and money to invent modern farming machinery. Very few people want to go back to hand-picking corn. In the same way, you may be able to automate many things you're doing currently. You may look back and be very glad it is now automated.

Hire Someone

Ok! You've figured out we need to hire an actual physical human being to do something.

Or have you?

There's a very high chance you instead want to hire an intermediary, that is, a middleman to help manage the person you want to hire. For example, you may think you need to hire a website designer for your flower shop. You're an expert in flowers, not websites. Most people aren't experts at websites, which is why so many people have terrible websites and bad relationships with their website suppliers. You may not have the skills to judge design talent, cost or what the underlying technology is.

Here you have two choices to find an intermediary between yourself and the website designer.

In the first instance, you can go to a website company rather than an individual. A company will have many people with multiple skills and reliability. They will have many web developers and so if one goes on vacation, others can take up the slack. If you hire just one freelancer, you don't have that fallback.

Second, you can find a project or product manager. This type of person may not have expertise around websites or flowers, but they are experienced managing these kinds of relationships. They will collect requirements from you (what do you want?) and commitments from your designer (when will they do it?) Then, every day or every week, they'll make sure everyone is on the same page.

Either way, it costs a little more money to have these intermediaries between you and the web developer/designer. But it can save you a lot more money, pain and valuable time down the road.

So – do you need an intermediary to help you? If you're hiring for a skill outside of what you do, it's a great idea to get some help from an intermediary, at least in the beginning. If you've hired 10 sales people before, you probably don't need help hiring number 11.

If you do need an intermediary, a project or product manager can be more than fine. You don't necessarily need an expert in the field you're working in to help manage the person. They can be a generalist, good at managing many types of projects. This can cut costs down over the long term.

Consider this; project manager can manage the hiring process as well.. You can hire a project manager and ask *them* to hire a great web designer using the criteria you set out. This again may seem to cost more time and money, but in many cases, will save you a lot of hassle (time and money). Do you want to look through 30 resumes, or can a project manager do that cheaper and quicker than you can?

Hire Someone: Part 2

Okay, Okay, the rubber is now meeting the road. You need people to do some work for you. And there are people in the market for your work. These people have several attributes to them:

- Experience
- Cost
- Location
- Culture
- Language
- Reliability
- Timing
- …

These tend to trade off against each other. Reliable, experienced people located near you will cost more than unreliable newbies on the other side of the planet.

Which attributes are important to *you?*

Arbitrage is buying something cheaply at one place or time and selling it more expensively at some later place.

For example, water may be cheap where you are, but next week (a change in time) there's a tornado and water prices go up. Or with the water example, it could be more expensive in the middle of the Sahara Desert (a change in location).

If you're willing to negotiate on different factors, you can typically get cheaper costs. Therefore, you should decide which ones are important to you.

Normally outsourcing is concerned only with location. Hiring someone far away is often cheaper monetarily, but it pays to think about how else it could be cheaper. The most interesting is time. If you're willing to wait a few weeks for work to be completed, you can often get it done more cheaply.

If it doesn't have to be the best work, you can be flexible on quality.

These things are all entangled. If a potential hire doesn't have a lot of experience, they will tend to charge less. On the other hand, they might take more time to complete the job. And in my experience, they will also tend to make mistakes, which cost more of *your* time.

Lastly, let's talk about trust.

Don't delude yourself. Trust comes over time and is complicated because we're human. You cannot and should not trust people straight away unless they're in a profession which heavily penalizes mistakes. You can usually trust a doctor for example because a position like this comes with an oath of trust, and if they screw up then they go to prison or have other major life problems.

Thus, when you're hiring on the internet for work you won't physically oversee, what level of trust do you need?

You'll want different levels of trust depending on what you're hiring for. If you're hiring an accountant, you'll want a higher level of trust. If you need creative work on a logo, you can be less stringent. There are three ways to get a comfortable level of trust working for you here:

1. Be in the same country. If your bookkeeper or accountant is in the same country as you, then you're under the same legal umbrella. Be careful though, people commit small fraud all the time and get away with it because it's usually more expensive to go after them than to move on.
2. Use secret sharing. Tools like QuickBooks Online allow an accountant to log in and do accountant things without having full access to your bank account. Be suspicious if they want more information than you think they need.

3. Use reputation. If someone has been doing this a long time with many clients, they're more likely to be trustworthy than the new guy. Outsourcing websites expose ratings and reviews of peoples past work that you can use to judge their trustworthiness.

Some things just aren't worth it. If you're going to lose sleep over trust, use someone near you with a real office you can visit and save outsourcing for things where trust isn't such an issue.

What do you need done from them?

When you hiring someone you typically want their time, a product, or both. Be clear about what you need.

If you have a question for a lawyer, you may need 10 minutes of their time on the phone. If you want a logo, you just want a logo as a final product. If you're iterating on something like a legal document, you want both. You want some time to talk about it with a lawyer, then a draft of the document, then time talk again about revisions.

Whether you need time or a product made is important, since there are different places to get these things. For example, 99designs (99designs.com) offers many end products where oDesk (odesk.com) offers more bespoke outsourcing.

Intellectual Property

Often you need the intellectual property (IP) such as copyrights, trademarks, database rights and anything else you can think of. You might assume that since you're paying someone to make something that you get the IP as part of the work. No. It doesn't work like that.

There are many fields where someone may have a brilliant idea, outside of work hours, that they later use. Does that "belong" to them or their employer? You need to have clarity over what you want to own. Usually this is "everything" but there may be exceptions.

There are "open" licenses which many photographers, writers, software engineers and others use. These licenses allow anyone to use the work (software code), so long as they adhere to some simple conditions. The biggest example is Wikipedia, but there are many others. Wikipedia allows you to use, modify and adapt articles so long as Wikipedia is attributed and the resulting work is licensed under the same terms.

Here's an example: You hire someone to automate a process for you with some software. You could keep that software you created to yourself, but maybe it isn't critical to you. If it is open source (other people can use the software code freely), you may find more developers willing to work on it. There are websites where developers share open software, like github.com.

Similarly, developers or artists may use open content and build on it. Let's say you hire someone to make some great slides for a presentation for you. They could buy art or use open photos for no cost. The open photos may be just as good and all they require is you have to say they're open on the slide.

Therefore, if you can be flexible with some of these ownership questions, you can save time and money. You should talk this through with those you hire (and a lawyer to be extra sure). If ownership is critical to you then keeping the IP rights may well be the better option.

Creativity and Understanding

Some tasks require creativity, like making a beautiful logo. Some require repetition, like calling 100 potential clients.

Which do you need?

It may seem clear, at first glance. But often it isn't. The perfectly obvious steps to follow, aren't obvious to anyone else but you The instructions for making a sandwich can get hilariously long when you list every detail like what type of knife to use and where to get it from.

For example, you may expect someone you hired to make cold calls, to introduce themselves and smile while making a phone call. You expect this because this is what you've been doing for decades and with great success. But, you can't assume a new hire works the same way; they may not share the same skills or culture.

Similarly, you may ask a new hire to repeat a task 100 times in a creative way. Let's say you make a leaflet for London and you ask someone to make 99 more leaflets for different cities. There are plenty of people out there who wouldn't know where to start with a task like that. Just picking 99 cities that would work for you may be a problem. They'll pick 99 in Europe but you wanted them worldwide. Things like that.

The examples may seem silly, but this *exact* kind of thing happens all the time! Therefore (especially at the beginning) be incredibly overly clear on tasks and check in frequently to stay on the same page, until trust and understanding is built. Over time you can back off.

The Most Important Factor

Here it is. When outsourcing: *Make sure they've done the kind of work you need before.*

Don't hire a lawyer to build you a jet engine. Don't hire a web designer to do your marketing copy.

Always hire someone who's done it before. If you want a painting, hire a painter.

Simple? Not quite so on the internet. You may have a great lawyer for contracts, but who's never done a rental agreement. Find a lawyer specializing in property and rentals. Or your web designer has never done sysadmin work. Find a sysadmin instead.

Skills may seem related or close but they aren't. If a potential hire has not done the task you're asking to be done before, then you're paying for them to learn how to do it. In small corner cases, this may work well for you. It may even be cheaper. But you're paying because you don't know how to do it, and if they don't know either then it's the blind leading the blind. So always find someone who knows, understands and has completed similar work in the past.

4 How to Find Freelancers

Okay, we've figured out *what* we want outsourced, and *who* we need. Now how and where do we find them?

You're dealing with human beings

Remember. These potential new hires might be on the internet, but they're still human. They might be charging pennies on the dollar, but they're still human. They might make mistakes, but well, they're human.

Your starting point in all this, is that you need a human being to help you. Not a computer or a robot. It's easy to lose track of this, so keep it in mind. These are people who have their own hopes and dreams, too.

Salary isn't always a strong predictor of value in outsourcing. For example: A $30k/year salary where you live, could buy a trailer park home. But that same salary to your potential outsourced worker, could buy them a top-floor, downtown apartment where they are. Don't assume salary has the same monetary value where you are as where your freelancer is.

Friction

Not long ago hiring people was expensive and time-consuming. Then parting ways was even more expensive and time-consuming. It still is, for many people on planet Earth.

The internet has changed much of this. It's quicker and cheaper than ever to hire and fire people. All this friction has gone away for hiring and firing, but we act like it hasn't. What I mean is, we still treat outsourcing in many ways like "real" employees.

Hiring online means communication and accountability can be a lot sharper than before. Most of the time, for example, there is no office politics in the way because there is no office. Communications are more constrained with remote workers. This isn't always a good thing. Many of us would prefer to hide behind office politics, then do any actual work.

Different types of work

We're going to go in-depth on three basic types of outsourcing.

1. Click Working. How and when to use Mechanical Turk (mturk.com).

2. Design Work. Competition to win your affection with 99Designs (99designs.com) and CrowdSpring (crowdspring.com).
3. Real Work. Leveraging UpWork (upwork.com) to hire real people.

Let's go!

5 Mechanical Turk: Click Working

Mechanical Turk allows you to take large numbers of repetitive tasks and farm them out to people all over the internet for pennies at a time. These people could live anywhere in the world. Here's an example: You have 1,000 photos and you want to know which contain cats and which contain dogs. With Mechanical Turk you can pay 1 penny per photo (as an example) and get the answers back in a spreadsheet. This is termed *click working*.

If the work you need to be done can be broken down in to simple tasks, then click working is for you.

These are the type of jobs where one person working alone would not usually be feasible. For example, you want to know the opening hours of 1,000 restaurants.

If you ask one person to do the entire task, then possibly they'll get bored. Not only that, it may not be possible in a reasonable amount of time. It also won't be easy to check if the work was done well.

On the other hand, what if you could hire 1,000 people to find one restaurant each? Or 100 to research 10 each? The resulting data on the restaurants is the same. Traditionally, you couldn't hire 1,000 people to complete this work, as the costs would be too high. Today, it's much more easy to achieve.

Enter Mechanical Turk at http://mturk.com/

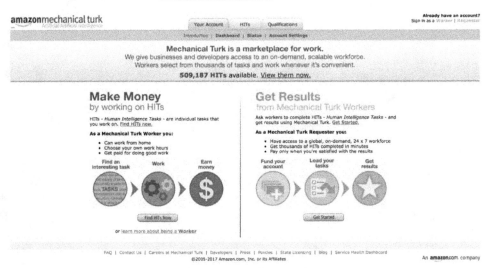

Figure 1: Mechanical Turk's home page

Click working is the most complex of the three options of outsourcing. This is because typically the employer will need some computer skills to distribute the work to the workers. For some simple tasks, spreadsheet knowledge is enough to get started, but for other things, HTML and other technologies are needed.

This isn't a technical book, and there are many guides on the internet for how to use Mechanical Turk. So, if you are technically-inclined then great, and if not, it's best to hire someone to help you here, like a project manager or technical advisor.

What we will talk about is how to think about and use Mechanical Turk at a higher level.

The biggest advantage of click working is repeatability. You can have a task repeated multiple times by different people. For ambiguous tasks – tasks with uncertain outcomes – this is very useful. For example, is the Mona Lisa smiling or frowning? An individual will give you one answer but if you ask 100 people you can get a statistical feeling for each possibility.

Most tasks are far more concrete, such as asking if a photo is of a dog or a cat and there is little dispute in the possible outcomes.

Mechanical Turk is very much a batch system. Think of it as having a large spreadsheet with a missing row. Imagine you are trying to find the phone number for 1,000 restaurants. You have a spreadsheet of 1,000 restaurants with their addresses but don't have their phone numbers. You send the spreadsheet off to Mechanical Turk, and it comes back with the empty phone number column now filled in for you.

One issue is ambiguity. You may ask Mechanical Turk to get a phone number, but the restaurant has two phone numbers. Or the restaurant is no longer in business. Another potential issue is that workers may have no way to tell you this, if you just asked for a phone number.

Therefore, the design of tasks can be very important. It's hard to predict what the problems with your tasks may be. They'll always surprise you. One way to avoid this, is to start with small samples of tasks first to work out the bugs.

A common mistake is to send all the items in a task you're working on off to Mechanical Turk and then check in a couple of days later. This means you'll come back to a lot of bad results. It's much better to send out a small sample first and pay a higher price per task in the beginning, so that you attract people to complete the work quickly. If you try with small samples first, you can work out the bugs you encounter early.

If you pay a high price per task (say 50 cents instead of 1 penny), you'll get results more quickly. Typically, you want to be quick so you can iterate. Just expect your first few tries to have serious problems with how you ask questions and the results you get back.

During this stage, if you come across a problem, you can quickly cancel the batch in Mechanical Turk. Then, you can go back and fix things before re-running the tasks. You may need to do this 2-3 times. But once it's done, you can send your full datasets to Mechanical Turk with a lot more confidence.

You can ask workers to do practically anything from making a phone call to writing a blog post. Feel free to offer low prices for a task to begin with, and then raise the offer price if you don't get results of the quality or speed you need. Experiment!

Consider another example: Your Amazon book wish list. Let's say you have hundreds of books and you'd like to know which of these are available at your library.

On one hand, you could manually go through your wish list yourself and type each title in to your libraries website search feature. Perhaps you have two windows open on your computer screen to make this process faster.

On the other hand, if you're clever you could write software to do this automatically for you (or hire someone to write it). But even if you have the skills to do so, Amazon doesn't make these lists available very easily, so it's more complicated than it looks.

Click working occupies a middle ground. Ideally a computer could automatically find your wish list items at your library, but for various reasons that is difficult to achieve. It's perhaps even more difficult to do manually.

With Mechanical Turk, you can send a request for the list of books. The question might look something like "What is the title and author of item number X on this list <clickable list URL>". This builds your list of books and authors.

The next task, using that data, is "Is this book <title>, by <author> available at my library? <library URL>". Then you'd get out a second spreadsheet of all these items from Mechanical Turk. And remember, the library can save you a few thousand dollars in buying books, so maybe this isn't a bad example!

Also, remember, there could be issues. For example, a book could be available but checked out at the library. It's best to try in small batches first to discover these little things. To make sure workers can report these edge cases.

And batches it is. It would be wonderful if you could make information flow through mechanical turk directly from one question to the next. You could ask "is a restaurant still open" and then if it is, "what is the main phone number" and so on. These tools don't exist like they should today, so think in batches of information, like filters.

Try to make the first task the one that filters out the most possible pieces of data. For example, imagine a task where we need to find restaurants addresses and website details. We could do one or the other task first as one step, and then the next with the filtered list. It will be filtered because some restaurants may be closed.

If we find the websites first by setting up one set of tasks, then it will be easier for subsequent workers to look on the website for the address of a restaurant. If we ask for the address first, then the address doesn't help people finding the website very much.

Therefore, considering which order to work on tasks can save time and money. Another alternative is to ask workers to do both in one task.

An aside

Mechanical Turk is often called MTurk and was started back in 2005. The name refers to a machine from a few hundred years ago which could play chess, but in reality a human was hidden inside it.

Mechanical Turk is great for things a computer can't quite do yet, but will soon. It wasn't so long ago that you'd use MTurk to look for things in photos that computers can do now for free.

Walkthrough of a simple task

Go to http://mturk.com/ and log in, which may require creating an account. Once that's done you'll find you can log in as a requester or worker. You want *requester* – someone who is going to pay for work. This is what the requester site looks like:

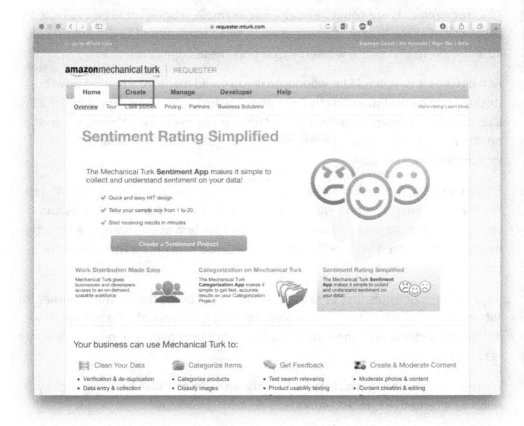

Click "Create" on the top menu to find the creation site:

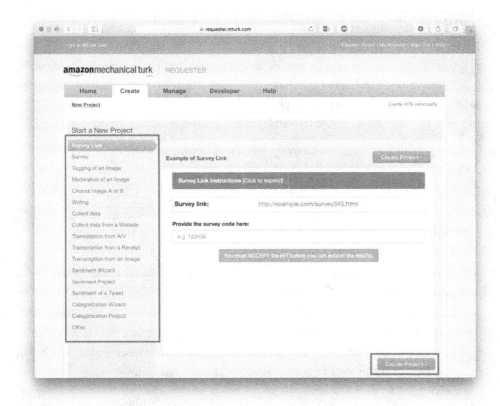

From here it's very self-explanatory and the site will walk you through how to create a task. Choose the project on the left that is closest to what you're trying to do. Then hit "Create Project". This will bring up the "Edit Project" screen. The important parts are "Setting up your HIT" and "Worker requirements".

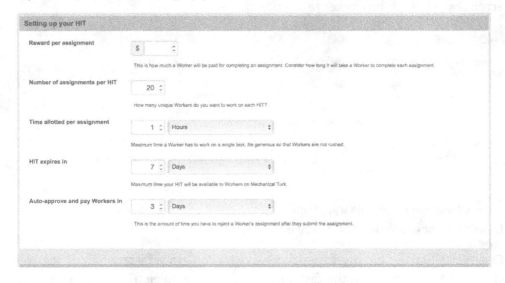

Setting up your HIT

A "HIT" is a row in your spreadsheet – a task to be done. Here we specify how much we want to pay per task (a penny, for example) as the "reward". The second field is slightly more confusing. It means how many times do you want the task repeated, by default 20 times. If you have a big list of pictures, you can have 20 people look at *each picture*. Maybe all 20 say it's a cat, maybe 2 think it's a dog.

We have many people look at the same item to get more opinions.

The next three fields go through timing.

- The first, the time allotted, is how long you give someone to do the work. Maybe looking at a cat takes 5 seconds but an hour is fine, maybe the worker gets distracted with a phone call then can come back.
- The second, (7 Days) refers to how long a task will live on Mechanical Turk before being deleted if nobody completed it.
- The last, (3 Days) means that if you do nothing after a worker completes a task, they will automatically be paid after the period you set. If you want to go through and look for bad work then you can, and deny the work. But you must do this within that 3 days, or change that timing here.

If you're paying a penny per task then looking back over completed work in detail may not be efficient. But for tasks where higher payouts occur, it can be worth checking the work is done well before paying.

Worker requirements

Scroll down to find the worker requirements:

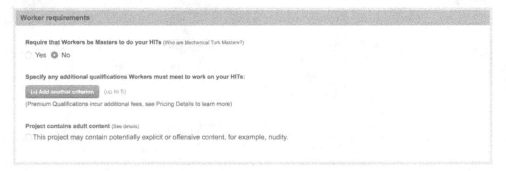

It's unlikely you need "Masters" unless you have complicated or very specialized tasks to do or where high accuracy is needed.

Essentially, Masters are pre-tested workers who you can set a test for and then be confident that if they pass the test they are capable of doing the task you set. This can reduce the amount of time and money you spend to check the tasks were done well.

For example, imagine a task where workers must look at pictures of fish and classify their species using a chart. With some training, they may be highly accurate, without training they are not. The "Masters" allows you to pre-filter by offering this training work, and then using these newly trained workers.

The important thing here is worker qualifications, and it usually comes down to location. The qualification options that pop up may be interesting or useful to you depending on the task. For example, you may want to run a survey of people in a specific income bracket.

Here are the default qualifications:

System Qualifications
    Location
    HIT Approval Rate (%) for all Requesters' HITs
    Number of HITs Approved
Premium Qualifications
    Primary Mobile Device - iPhone
    Primary Mobile Device - Android
    US Political Affiliation - Conservative
    US Political Affiliation - Liberal
    US High School Graduate
    Marital Status - Married
    Parenthood Status
    Voted in 2012 US Presidential Election
    Tablet Owner
    Smoker
    Car Owner
    US Bachelor's Degree
    Handedness - Left
    Handedness - Right
    Marital Status - Single
    Marital Status - Divorced
    US Graduate Degree
    Household Income - Less than $25,000
    Household Income - $25,000 - $49,999
    Household Income - $50,000 - $74,999
    Household Income - $75,000 - $99,999
    Household Income - $100,000 or more
    Current Residence - Owned
    Current Residence - Rented
    Single Family Home Resident
    Employment Status - Full time (35+ hours per week)
    Employment Status - Part time (1-34 hours per week)
    Employment Status - Unemployed
    Primary Internet Device - Desktop
    Primary Internet Device - Laptop
    Primary Internet Device - Smartphone or Tablet
    Blogger
    Military experience

Location is an important qualification for many tasks and usually comes down to finding people in your country. If you're in France, you probably want French people to phone up restaurants and ask for their phone number.

These qualifications can all be changed later, so have a look around and move on. If your qualification settings somehow lead to a problem with tasks, you can come back and re-run the whole task with different qualifications.

Design Layout

Next is the "Design Layout". This is what the worker will see.

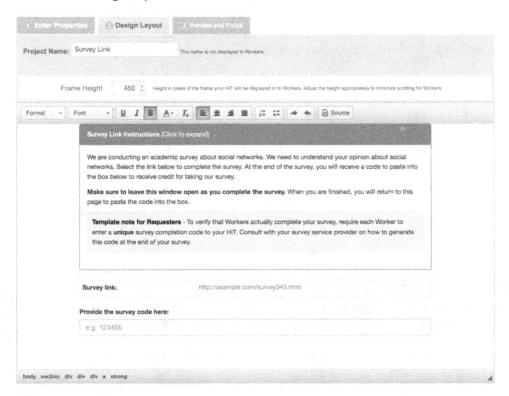

The default is quite telling – it's a link to a survey. So, the worker looks at this page, then clicks to go to *another* page (the "example.com" link above) to complete the actual survey. This second page gives them a code to use when complete, and then they enter this code back on Mechanical Turk.

In this setup, you can use any website or tool you wish, and Mechanical Turk is effectively just the billing platform for finding people to complete the task.

As for the security code you give a worker, you can use the same one every time. For many tasks, setting up a code system to check who is who and so on is too complicated. You can give workers a random code that's automatically generate or give every worker the same code and it'll probably work just as well as giving unique codes for each task. From the workers' perspective, they have a valid code and will behave as if it's important, even if you never use it.

If you're paying more than a few pennies per task, then this might not work well as you can lose money.

Essentially this code system exists to prevent fraud. A worker on Mechanical Turk must validate completed work by being given a code on the third-party website then use that code to close the task on Mechanical Turk. If they don't have a code then they have no proof they completed the work.

Usually nobody has the time or energy to try to defraud these simple systems, if the amount of money they'd gain is small.

Finishing up

In the design editor, you can build any kind of page you like, put in fields, questions and data from a spreadsheet. Feel free to try some of the example templates Amazon provides to see how different tasks can be farmed out to workers.

When you're done, you preview, finish and pay. Then you can set the task "live" and watch results come back in. Remember, the more money you pay, the quicker the results will be.

The output is a big spreadsheet with your results. The results will also include other columns like what time the task was completed. Your job now is to look through and see if you got what you expected, and if not, rework the task to account for any issues.

A good practice is to leave an optional field for the worker to make a note of anything that didn't work or may need improvement.

A full investigation of all these things and how to write the HTML is too technical for this book and would result in dozens of screenshots. If you need help you can hire someone technical or drop me an email.

6 Design Competitions

CrowdSpring (crowdspring.com) and 99Designs (99designs.com) are two of the most well-known websites for running competitions for work, mostly design work.

Since there are two websites mentioned here and they're similar to each other we'll skip the screenshot-by-screenshot walk through. It's best to read through this with one of them open, and work through the process of creating a competition.

Let's say you need a logo designed. You could hire one person directly, but maybe they don't come up with anything you like. With crowdsourcing sites, you get design ideas from many people and then choose the one you like the best.

Competition websites have expanded far beyond just logos to websites, book covers, packaging and full brand identity packages.

If you're not a designer (it'd be puzzling why you'd use these if you *are*) then you need to know how to communicate what you want to a designer. We call this a design brief, and a designer will love you if you put one together for them.

Design Brief

A design brief is just a list of questions about what you want. Designers are asked all the time for "a cool logo" but, let's be honest, that isn't much to go on. Below is a simple, example design brief. It's a set of questions which you answer about your project to try and communicate the type of design work you're looking for. The example is done for an imaginary organic farm which needs a logo:

- What **must** the design communicate?
  - Green fields or farming
  - Honesty
  - The farm's name (Bob's Organic Farm)
- What **mustn't** the design communicate?
  - "Big corporation"
  - Toxic or industrial food
- What thoughts/feelings should it communicate?
  - Warmth
  - Honesty
- What thoughts/feelings should it **not** communicate?
  - Coldness
  - Ugly

- Who is it targeted at
  - Busy moms
- ...and so on

You can find example design briefs on CrowdSpring and 99Designs. These sites also have their own design questionnaires they'll guide you through.

To a designer, typically the more information from you is better. More information allows a designer understand more about what you're trying to achieve.

What to Pay

Once you've described your project (on one of the competition sites) you'll be invited to pay extra money for more exposure to your project. You'll be asked for money to feature your project on the competition website. Typically, this isn't worth the money and can be skipped. The more money you pay the final designer, the better.

Arbitration

Designers want to be paid, but you usually have the option to not pay anyone if there are no designs you like. If there's a problem finalizing a design once you've chosen one you like, your dispute can be mediated by the competition website themselves who will step in as an arbiter.

This is similar to eBay disputes between buyers and sellers where eBay steps in an resolves the issue.

You can usually waive your right to this arbitration. This means that *someone* will get paid even if you have a problem. If you do this, it will attract more designers since they can be confident they'll get paid if selected and won't be stuck in any arbitration proceedings.

How Much to Spend

Pay as much as you can budget for your design work. Usually the design of your materials is the "public face" of your product or service and it's important to make a great first impression. Cheaper design work tends to show badly.

You can usually go with the defaults on most of the settings when creating a competition (how long the competition should be, price, advertising options...).

Judging Entries

As the competition starts you'll start to get entries, and this is when the work for you begins. Typically, the early designs are poor quality. Don't be discouraged by this as they get dramatically better over time. The task for you is to provide honest and timely feedback.

When you provide feedback, all existing and potential designers in the marketplace see it. This is useful to them to hear what you like and don't like. You need to give a 1-5 star rating for each entry and can write a comment about it. It's important to be honest and as descriptive as possible so that people can start to give you more of what you want to see, and less of what you don't.

The quicker you are to give feedback, the quicker you will get revised results. If you delay, people will assume you're not interested in the work. This is very bad. At least once a day, go through all the entries and provide feedback until the competition is done.

In your comments, it's important to reference where the logo will be used. Design for a business card can be different than for the front of a building as they have different constraints. Usually logos these days are for websites, so be clear where it will be used, giving designers a frame of reference.

Example

Here's a typical example of a logo project with entries from many designers:

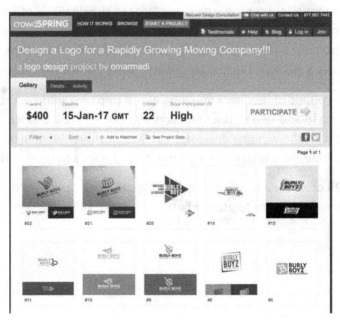

Notice that some designers provide photo-realistic mock-ups on business cards, while others are using the logo image itself. There are some color or format options in the entry image itself.

Your job is to look through your entries and score them, with as much feedback as possible, as often as possible. Don't be afraid of being honest.

If you're new to design, here are some things that can help you.

- Read a book on design. The principles aren't that hard, and there are many interesting books out there such as The Non-Designers Design Book by Robin Wiliams.
- Look for simplicity. Simpler is better in any design.
- Look at it from a distance. Look at the logo on your screen, nice and large by zooming in with your browser. Now walk 10 or 20 paces away and look back at the screen. Can you still read the text? Can you understand the design?
- Squint. If you squint, it's like looking at the logo through fog or rain, or if you only get a second to look at it. How does it look when you squint at it? Remember – some people will only see your logo briefly.
- Ask strangers to look and see if they can figure out what it is. If a logo clearly says "Los Gatos" for them, that's great. But is it a restaurant or the local vet? It should both say what it is and communicate what *type* of thing it is.

Design entry submissions typically pick up closer to the deadline of your project. Toward the end, a designer can come and see what everyone else has submitted (and your responses) and use both to figure out what they'd produce. Because they have this as a guide, it means the quality of the entries goes up over time.

After multiple rounds of feedback you'll be asked to pick a winner. You may also pick a runner-up in addition to the main winner. You'll have a chance to communicate with the winning designer. You will approve the final images before all is said and done, plus select various formats and colors to receive them in.

A price of $199 or so for a logo is great value (a designer can easily cost ten times this). Consider paying more to attract better talent for better design.

7 UpWork: Hiring Real People

UpWork is a marketplace for hiring remote workers. For almost anything you can think of, from lawyer to project managers to translators. You can use UpWork to find an electronics engineer and UpWork will handle the hiring process. UpWork will act as a marketplace, matching freelancers and employers. They also take care of payments between you and people you hire.

Mechanical Turk and design competitions are both anonymous crowds of people you can leverage at great value. With UpWork you'll get personal.

There tricky parts are all over the place in UpWork. To avoid wasting time and money spinning your wheels, let's take this step-by-step.

First – we're going to hire a real actual person to work with. Mechanical Turk and the design competition sites hide a lot of this complexity from us.

We should know what kind of person we want to hire.

UpWork is a global marketplace for every skill type possible. Ask yourself some basic questions before you get started:

- Do you care what country they're in?
    - Far away countries are typically cheaper
    - Some countries have a culture of creativity
    - Some countries have a culture of engineering discipline
    - Some countries have poor internet connectivity
    - Be careful, many ex-pats are on UpWork in every country, so don't restrict yourself unnecessarily
- Do you care what language they speak?
    - Not just with you, but perhaps with other team members
    - Remember many countries have multiple languages, like French and English-speaking Canada for example
- Do you care what time zone they are in?
    - Countries on the other side of the planet work when you're asleep. Your morning is their evening
    - Countries north and south of you share your work times, perhaps approximately
- Do you care how you communicate?
    - Email, IM, skype, bug tracking, project management…

Try to get a general feel for which aspects you're flexible on and which you're not. It can be useful to make a checklist of these items to refer to in future, when you hire again.

Before we go any further let's make one thing clear – you'll need to experiment. You won't hire the perfect person on the first try, or at least it's unlikely. It's ok to try someone for a week and then let them go and try again. Don't be discouraged if it doesn't work out immediately.

Countries

Every country has thin, fat, smart, stupid and any other type of person. What shapes them is the education and other experience they receive. So, remember that stereotypes are just that, stereotypes.

If you limit your workers by country you're also missing out on Ex-pats. There are British people in China and Chinese people in Britain for example.

Here are some educational and cultural differences that I've found in the many years of using UpWork (and its predecessors eLance and oDesk):

- Some countries encourage conformity and rote learning. These can be great for repetitive tasks or processes that are already clear
- Some countries have strong engineering cultures
- Some countries have strong foreign language skills despite low wages
- Some countries make it illegal to work for foreign companies. This means the risk takers from those places are on UpWork

These things – education, culture and language are the results of historical accidents. They're often counter-intuitive. It helps to remember that the person you hire may come from a different culture and educational background and this can be a great thing, since their different perspective can open new ways of achieving goals.

Languages

The obvious first issue is whether you share a language, and what level of fluency you need from a worker.

But there is a wrinkle – many people are more fluent writing than speaking! Therefore, IM can often work great. IM can be better for other reasons too - speaking on skype can also use more bandwidth which may be at a premium at their end; not everywhere has great internet.

Time zones

If you don't need to communicate often with your UpWork hire, then time zone differences won't be much of an issue.

The big thing to think about is wasting time. If a developer, say, does some work and either goes in the wrong direction or gets stuck, how much time is lost?

Time (which costs money) can be wasted in two ways. The first is when your freelancer keeps working on something that isn't relevant before you catch it. The second is in waiting. Waiting for you to explain something they don't understand or a bug which needs to be fixed for example.

Because of time zone differences, these periods can be inflated. Let's say you catch a software bug on a Thursday. You write is up as an issue and they get it late Friday. They get to work on it Monday, thus having a fix for you on Tuesday. You look at it on Wednesday. That's almost a week from your perspective! Or in the other case, they could be working on the wrong thing for 2-3 days before you catch it.

This is important when you're iterating a project. If the project is more stand-alone or 'fire and forget' then it may not be an issue for you. But watch out, many 'simple' pieces of work can get complicated quickly.

Being in a similar time zone can help in some cases. North America has similar time zones to South America. Europe and much of Africa are in similar time zones. Just be careful, it can get tiring having early or late meetings all the time to keep track of people. For example, even a 2-hour time zone difference can mean regular calls at 9pm if your worker has another day job and you can't talk during dinner.

Communication Tools

Communicating with outsourced workers is difficult. You're working with a new person in a different time zone who speaks a different native language. Even in the best of circumstances that can be trying. Your remote workers will very much appreciate concise guidelines on how and when to communicate.

You need a shared understanding of where the project is at and where it's going for anything other than trivial cases. One tool you can use is Trello (trello.com), which is a shared board with cards which can be in different columns:

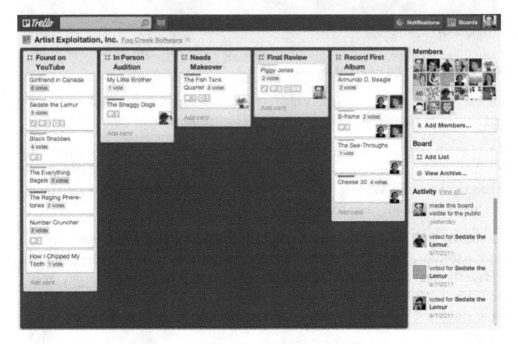

Trello allows you to invite people to a shared board. The board contains grouped tasks in vertical columns. You can have a column of bugs and another for fixed bugs which you and your workers can edit.

There are many other options for keeping on the same page. For software projects, GitHub and GitLab are good choices to store the code and create bugs. You create a bug or task such as "login broken" and describe the issue. Your developer can comment on this and close the bug as needed.

Your responsibility is to double-check things are done as communicated. Perhaps ask your developer to mark a bug as fixed, and then you formally close it when you're satisfied.

Immediate Communication

As well as the project status, you need other tools for more immediate communication.

Skype is a popular tool for instant messaging (IM), video or voice. Almost all contractors will have Skype. Remember to turn it off or mute your phone at night, as it's normal for workers to IM you at 3am and then you respond when you're available.

For sharing files, you'll most likely want to use Dropbox. The reason for this is its widespread use and the fact it works on every operating system (Skype does too).

If you use OneDrive or iCloud Drive, as examples, you may find it difficult for people using Linux or Windows. Remember – the more flexible you are, the easier it is to find and hire people. If you strictly need people to run a specific operating system or tool, then you cut down the number of workers you can potentially hire.

If you have more than one person working on a project, then group tools will be important. Group Skype chats only go so far. For group communication, the market leader is Slack (slack.com). It's a group chat room that works on practically any computer or phone. Though now there are many clones of Slack available such as HipChat.

UpWork itself has some basic communication tools which you'll use during the hiring process. They're fine for starting with, but you'll want better tools as you go on. For example, UpWork doesn't currently support video communication.

Project Managers

It may seem counter-intuitive, but whoever you hire, consider hiring a project manager first instead of the actual worker.

They can insulate you a lot from of the day-to-day complexities, the and ups and downs. A good project manager is a good middle man, sitting between you and the contractor. It costs a little more money, but can save you a lot of time.

If you've hired for a role before, or know the role inside-out (say you're a designer hiring a designer) then hire them directly.

If not, then a project manager can advertise, interview and hire people for you. They can keep the new hires on track and communicate with you when and how you want to. They'll deal with the random questions at 3am. This can save you a **lot** of pain. And you can learn from them how they do it, too.

The Hiring Process

Let's assume you've gone to upwork.com, have created an account and want to post a job. Here we'll walk through the hiring screen. First, choose the category of work you need and name the job:

Post a Job

Reuse previous job

Select previous job

Choose a category and subcategory

Please select...

Describe the Job

Name your job posting

EXAMPLE: Need Help Developing a Powerpoint Presentation for a Family Reunion

A fun name is entirely ok, for example "Engineering Ninja".

Next, you need to add a description:

The description is where it immediately gets complicated. If you're having trouble writing a captivating summary of the work, look around at other job postings.

Be as specifc as possible in your posting. The more detail you put in, the better able workers will be to see if they're a good fit for you.

Here's my big tip which will save you a **lot** of time: A few sentences in to your job summary say this: "Please mention the word 'hippopotamus' in your application".

Here's why – half or more of the people who apply for your job won't read the application. They're looking for work and applying to every job possible. You don't usually want these workers.

Later, when you read through all the applications, just trash anyone who didn't mention 'hippopotamus'. This alone will save you hours of time. Pick a different word of your own. I've tried 'banana' and that works well.

Feel free to include images, sketches, mock ups or any other design documents in the job description. Use the "Attach file" feature for this.

Are you worried about someone 'stealing' your idea? Don't be. There are zillions of ideas on UpWork every day. Worrying about theft only slows down the execution of your idea. You need people to implement your idea and get going! And I bet you that someone, somewhere, has had your idea already and is just sitting on it.

Lastly, select the type of project (one-time, ongoing or not sure). Don't feel constrained by this, you can change it later.

If you scroll down, the hiring page continues:

Rate and Availability

How would you like to pay?

Pay by the hour

Desired Experience Level

$	$ $	$ $ $
Entry Level	Intermediate	Expert

How long do you expect this job to last?

6+	3-6	1-3		
More than 6 months	3 to 6 months	1 to 3 months	Less than 1 month	Less than 1 week

What time commitment is required for this job?

More than 30 hrs/week	Less than 30 hrs/week	I don't know yet

You need to choose how you want to pay. There are two options:

1. Pay by the hour. This is usually best and is like hiring a regular contractor. UpWork lets you see what your workers are doing via screenshots-- we'll get to this later.
2. Pay a fixed price. This is for one-off projects that are well defined. Personally, I usually avoid this as it can lead to conflict. Inevitably fixed projects underestimate the actual time needed and bugs happen. If you keep asking for more time and effort, and this happens very often, your worker won't get paid more. They'll disappear, stop working on your project or ask for more money. You'll have to find someone else to continue or finish the project, or, pay the original worker.

Next, pick the "Intermediate" experience level. Whichever experience level you pick, you'll still get all types of workers applying for your job.

Next pick the job length, to the best of your knowledge.

Now you need to pick the time requirement. This is more important. You're signaling if you want someone full-time or not. Don't say you want someone for 6 months full-time if you're not sure about it, it's not fair to your worker.

Scrolling down, you have more preferences to indicate:

Freelancer Preferences

Do you want freelancers to find and apply to your job?

◉ Freelancers using Upwork.com and public search engines can find this job.

○ Only Upwork users can find this job.

○ Only freelancers I have invited can find this job.

Do you have freelancers in mind that you would like to invite?

Select freelancers

Preferred Qualifications

Specify the qualifications you're looking for in a successful application. Freelancers may still apply if they do not meet your preferences, but they will be clearly notified that they are at a disadvantage.

Add Qualifications

You have three choices on how you allow freelancers to find you job posting:

1. **Totally public.** The inclusion of search engine traffic has never helped in my experience: Workers tend to find work on UpWork, not searching Google.
2. **Only UpWork.** This is what I generally pick. This blocks search engine traffic, which I don't see any benefit from. Perhaps someone will find my job in 3 years on some search engine and link it to me, which I probably don't want.
3. **Only workers you invite.** If you have already found someone on UpWork, this is a good choice. Or if you're hiring someone again. Typically, you won't use this a lot since with option 2 above, you can both find people yourself and let them find you.

Next you choose qualifications. If you click the "Add Qualifications" button, it opens up a list similar to Mechanical Turks qualifications list and looks like this:

Preferred Qualifications

Specify the qualifications you're looking for in a successful application. Freelancers may still apply if they do not meet your preferences, but they will be clearly notified that they are at a disadvantage.

Hide Qualifications	
Freelancer Type	No preference ⌄
Job Success Score [?]	90% Job Success & up ⌄
Rising Talent [?]	Include Rising Talent ⌄
Hours Billed on Upwork	Any amount ⌄
Location	Any location ⌄
English Level (self-assigned)	Any level ⌄
Group	No preference ⌄

I rarely use qualification because I don't want to restrict applicants straight away. I may have some pre-conception about restricting people, say by location. It usually turns out to be wrong. For example, I may believe that Romanians typically have much better English than Ukrainians and exclude them. But if workers don't have good English, they tend not to be on UpWork in the first place. I advise you to leave the qualifications open to start with. You can always filter later.

We're almost done setting up hiring. Now scroll down to choose screening questions and a cover letter:

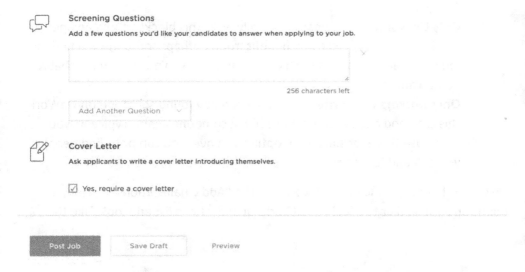

I usually leave the screening question blank, but it can be useful. If you're hiring for a task you know well; because you've hired for it before or you yourself do it, then this can be useful. But if you are hiring for a skill outside of your area, you typically won't know the right questions to ask anyway.

Ask for a cover letter. Most applicants will copy and paste one they already have for every job they apply for.

Post your job and you're done!

Don't worry about making sure the job posting is perfect. You can edit it later or just delete it and post a new job if necessary. The key here is to get experience of the whole process of hiring so that it becomes easy to do – you're not committing to hire anyone.

Interviewing

Very quickly, you'll get applicants to your job.

Many of these applicants, especially the first ones, operate on a "spray and pray" mentality. They apply for every possible job they see, without reading the description. This means you have no idea if they can do the work you are asking for and you need to filter them out. Remember my "Hippopotamus" suggestion? This is where using a semi-hidden word like that helps.

Wait a day or so before you start to weed out applicants. This lets the Earth rotate and people all over the world have a chance to look at and apply for your job.

This is what the screen for reviewing proposals looks like:

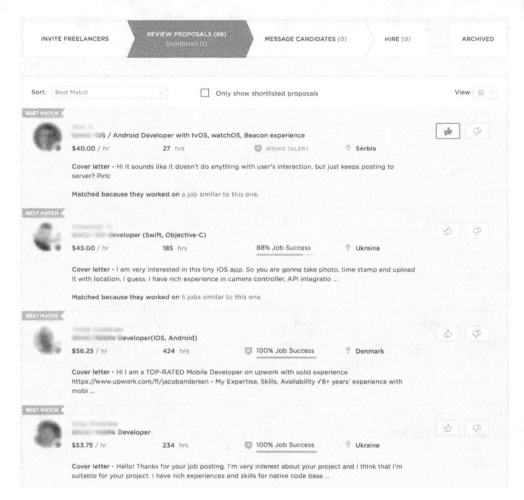

Sort: Best Match   ☐ Only show shortlisted proposals   View ▤

BEST MATCH

iOS / Android Developer with tvOS, watchOS, Beacon experience
$40.00 / hr   27 hrs   RISING TALENT   Serbia

Cover letter - Hi It sounds like it doesn't do anything with user's interaction, but just keeps posting to server? Piric

Matched because they worked on a job similar to this one.

BEST MATCH

Developer (Swift, Objective-C)
$45.00 / hr   185 hrs   88% Job Success   Ukraine

Cover letter - I am very interested in this tiny iOS app. So you are gonna take photo, time stamp and upload it with location, I guess. I have rich experience in camera controller, API integratio ...

Matched because they worked on 5 jobs similar to this one.

BEST MATCH

Developer(iOS, Android)
$56.25 / hr   424 hrs   100% Job Success   Denmark

Cover letter - Hi I am a TOP-RATED Mobile Developer on upwork with solid experience. https://www.upwork.com/fl/jacobandersen - My Expertise, Skills, Availability ✓8+ years' experience with mobi ...

BEST MATCH

Developer
$53.75 / hr   234 hrs   100% Job Success   Ukraine

Cover letter - Hello! Thanks for your job posting. I'm very interest about your project and I think that I'm suitable for your project. I have rich experiences and skills for native code base ...

I've blurred out the applicants faces and names and these are 4 of 40+ applicants I received for a job.

The first thing to do is to get a feel for the type of applicants by sorting them in various ways. Look at the hourly rate, the number of hours worked on UpWork, their success ratio (how many previous jobs were a success) and country.

The "Sort" box has six options:

1. Best Match. This is the default. UpWork will show you a variety of candidates. Notice from the above screenshot we have a wide range of candidates in location, hours worked and hourly price.
2. Newest Applicants. The last people to apply, ignore this at first.
3. Oldest Applicants. The first people to apply, you can ignore this.
4. Highest Hourly Rate. This is key. Higher paid people tend to do a better job and have more hours of work experience.

5. Lowest Hourly Rate. Worth a look, but typically these workers do not have a good history. Sometimes you can find someone good who's bidding low so that they can get a job and some feedback on the UpWork platform.
6. Most Hours Worked. This is a very useful metric. People with many hours will tend to be far better than others, as they have the experience and have been proven by working for other people.

What should you look for first?

- The Cover Letter will tell you instantly if the worker has read your job description. Notice that only two of the top four applicants in my example project wrote anything specific. These two are worth looking at more deeply.
- Excessively low hourly rates and low number of logged hours tend to be bad.
- Anything other than 100% job success is an issue. There can be good reasons for having less than 100% which you can explore later, but I suggest starting with people who have 100%.
- Are they from an outsourcing firm? My preference is to work with individuals rather than those that are part of a team, but you may find differently. Teams tend to add friction and over promise what they can work on.
- Do they claim every possible skillset? Workers who focus on a small number of skills tend to be better than those who claim to know how to do everything.
- Anyone claiming that they "carefully read your proposal" almost certainly did not.

Having looked through all the applicants, it's time to start filtering. Go through the whole list and click the "thumbs up" and "thumbs down" for those you do and don't feel will do a good job. Don't worry, the applicants won't see this.

This is our first pass at filtering down the list of people who've applied for your job. Aim for about one thumbs up in every 3-10 applicants. When you have a reasonable list, say 12 workers, it's time to dig deeper. Don't worry, you can always go back and look at the ones you initially passed on.

If you're short of time, then sort the list by highest hourly rate, and hire the top person straight away. Remember, you can try them for a few days and move on if it doesn't work out. You could also have them build a part of the project as a test to begin with.

You can also hire multiple people. Sort the list by lowest hourly rate and hire two or three people for the same job, or different parts of it.

You can't expect all of them to work out first try. This gives you a chance to see the work of your top choices. Once you find the right person, you can work with them again and again in the future. In the end, you only find the best people by trying them and seeing if they work out.

If you're less sure of who to pick first and want more detail on a certain applicant, click on their profile. A panel will open with more information on them, their full work history and so on.

Jump straight to the section marked 'Work History and Feedback'. You get two things from this – first scan the descriptions and number of stars assigned. Look for good feedback, and lots of feedback from different people. Also, notice the hourly rate. Often it will be lower than what they quoted you, and you can ask for a lower rate because of this.

The "Portfolio" is most useful for designers, where they showcase their work. For other jobs, skip it, as the portfolio there can often just be descriptive about what the worker *can* do.

The other things like the Overview, the Tests they completed, Employment History and so on are interesting to skim, but all of them can be manipulated.

You can also message the applicant or have a skype chat to gain more clarity. Generally, I just hire someone. The tradeoff is, I could spend 2 or 4 hours thinking and interviewing people or I could hire someone and spend a little money instead. I've always found that just spending a little money is by far the best and quickest way to find out if someone is a good fit.

Choose someone, hire them, and set up a time to chat about the project. You can do this over IM or skype, it's up to you.

Watching your Worker

In the final step of hiring, you'll be asked if you want to allow "manual time" on the contract. Manual time allows a worker to claim that they did some work for some specified amount of time. Until you're comfortable with UpWork, avoid allowing manual time because you need to be able to track what work is being done.

UpWork has an alternative tracking system which takes a screenshot of your workers screen every ten minutes. It also tracks the amount of mouse and keyboard usage. You can see what it looks like here:

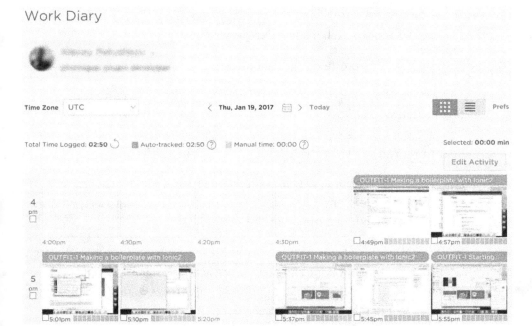

This screenshot shows two hours where a worker did about 20 minutes of work (the two top screenshots) in the first hour and 50 minutes in the second. You can click on these to get a feel for what they were working on.

The green progress bars beneath each screenshot show how much keyboard and mouse activity happened during that 10-minute segment.

Once someone is hired, you can reach this tracking screen by clicking "Work Diary". I advise you to do this now and again. The most common thing that happens is that a worker will switch to a different job without telling the UpWork tool. When this happens, you are paying for someone else's work. It's a simple and honest mistake.

This record allows you some good insight in to where the time (and therefore money) is being spent on your project.

Iteration

At the start of your project, you should be checking in at least daily or perhaps hourly. This is a step-by-step or *iterated* approach where you break the project up in to a series of simple tasks.

The biggest mistake in outsourcing is to create a grand design for a project and hand it off to workers. If you do this, and many people do, don't be surprised if you come back in a month and the wrong thing has been built.

It's **very** important to start small and check in as often as possible. To begin with you check in very often to catch if something is wrong.

As time goes on one of two outcomes will happen:

1. The work relationship doesn't work out and you need to part ways (more on this below).
2. You gain confidence over the work and your relationship, you build trust over time. You can start to back off and check in less frequently.

Workers can get delayed or underestimate how much time they have available to work on your project. There are many other reasons for something going wrong, and the sooner you catch it and move on the better.

When you're iterating, set clear expectations and goals. Agree on them with your hire. You can also agree what happens in different scenarios. For example, you may agree that a specific feature must be done by tomorrow, and if not, another team member needs to take over or help.

Try not to change the goals too much as you iterate, or you can end up never finishing. If you've never done project management work before, this can be a good time to read up on how it works, or hire someone to help. Managing freelancers is a skill you will develop, and you shouldn't expect to be great at it straight away.

Staying on top of your job by iterating and having clear goals, and finding new people to work with if results aren't happening, will avoid the main pitfall of Outsourcing-- You won't come back in a month, thousands of dollars poorer with no results.

Parting Ways
So, it didn't work out.

Don't hang around waiting to move on. Firing someone isn't pleasant of course, but, it's best for everyone to move forward if something isn't working out. Nobody ever said "oh I wish I'd kept that person around another month before firing them". Instead, most people are relieved and wish they'd done it earlier. The sooner you move on, the best for everyone.

UpWork makes hiring and firing as easy as clicking on buttons. Reducing complexity and increasing speed is useful almost always. But it can also allow you to make cold decisions so before you click "fire" check you've made an effort:

- Were you clear in the beginning and as you iterated about expectations?
- Did you communicate clearly that performance wasn't what you needed?
- Did you offer the worker a chance to fix things?
- Is this worker better suited to another role you have?

Remember – they're still a human being with hopes and dreams just like you.

When leaving feedback, try to think of the "glass half full" idea. That is, look on the bright side. It may not have worked out for you, but leaving positive feedback allows the freelancer to try again with someone else.

Another tip – you don't need to wait until one worker is fired before hiring another. The new one may need help from the old one for a transition period, for example. You can stop the existing work, find someone new and then connect the two.

This is an important point. If you can get out of the way and let your workers communicate between each other (perhaps cc'ing you), you may save substantial time money and stress.

In Sum

We've explored the full cycle of hiring and working with people using UpWork. It's time for you to experiment and hire some people to see what works for you. Let me know how it goes.

8 Closing

Other options

Here are a few other options that can help you find people and get things done.

Google Surveys (https://www.google.com/analytics/surveys/) offers a cheap way to gather data from many people. You can use this to gather information on a market instead of using Mechanical Turk.

Pre-built templates can often take you quite far. Envato Market (envato.com)has many market places for digital work, such as Theme Forrest (themeforest.net) for Wordpress (wordpress.org) templates. Wordpress is an open source blogging platform that can be turned in to just about anything from a blog to a web store using templates.

Envato has other marketplaces for photos, videos, audio and much more.

Connecting the pieces

Outsourcing gets very interesting when you connect the various pieces we've talked about in this book together.

Here are some examples:

- Buy a Wordpress template and find a worker to make minor improvements to it, rather than starting from scratch or doing it yourself.
- Hire project managers to hire and work with freelancers, avoiding all the day-to-day issues yourself.
- Start a design competition for a logo, pick the best 5 images, then hire people on Mechanical Turk to vote for the best one of the 5.
- Build app templates with an outsourced team, then resell these on a marketplace.
- Take an open source piece of software or design, hire someone to improve it and release the improvements. This saves all the initial work required to build a tool, if there is one that's close but not quite right.
- Hire freelancers to automate an existing process you have.

Have fun and experiment! You might be surprised by how much time and money you can save by putting outsourcing tools together like this. You can use this saved energy to build more things you need or just go on vacation.